Praise for D&I Has Died

"This book takes a very educational style to linking inclusion and the business metric of profit. Readers are carefully guided through the history that led up to multiple governmental workplace acts of protection for marginalized groups. Then, Desmund Adams demonstrates how pervasive the issue is from the executive ranks right up to the board of director level.

Thankfully, multiple studies have been conducted that link profit to inclusion and innovation. Diversity & Inclusion, as a normative, needs to be turned on its head and this book is just the wake-up call necessary."

The Honorable Roderick R. Paige
Former United States Secretary of Education 2001–2005

"Socially responsible recruitment needs to be a way of life for businesses to thrive and compete in the global marketplace. The days of "checking the box" to ensure a diverse slate of candidates based on gender and race only are over. Inclusivity MUST be the driver in attracting, developing and retaining talent. The ease of accessing data as a result of the digital transformation will unmask the true fabric of a business and those left standing will be most successful based on any measurable financial metric because of their actions in leveraging inclusion."

Mike Wright
Former Global Chief Human Resources Officer
Covanta, Russell 1000 Company

"Desmund has tapped into a main artery regarding corporate Diversity & Inclusion (D&I) recruitment with his provocative book—intent versus impact. Many of the original tenets of corporate D&I were built upon good intentions, but have yet to produce the types of sustained results desired. Its very goal has frequently been unattainable simply because of misaligned approaches.

Desmund's emphasis on socially responsible recruitment provides a thought provoking viewpoint by which D&I recruitment should be considered and advanced. By considering and adopting the fresh perspective this book brings to the D&I discussion, leaders can produce improved operations, more engaged staff, and an ever-increasing bottom line."

Bernie Frazier, SPHR
Author, National Professional Development Speaker
& Trainer, Former Healthcare Talent Acquisition Leader

"In the new book "D&I Has Died," executive recruiter and management consultant Desmund Adams deconstructs the diversity-and-inclusion movement to reveal its innate failures and recommends a new model that will accomplish the original (laudable) goals of D&I, AND drive profits to the bottom line, through "socially responsible recruitment." This book must be read by everyone in management with responsibility for remaking the demographic balance of a firm's management team or board of directors. Without the guidance contained in these pages, you may be doomed to repeat the mistakes of the past and miss the "profit opportunity," including improved workforce innovation, in a "social responsibility" recruitment effort. "Fight for an inclusive workforce!" Make this your battle cry and have the rationale to support it after reading this text by Adams', a tour-de-force for inclusion practices in the 21st century. "

Chuck Standfuss, J.D.
Human Resources Director and Past Trial Lawyer

D&I Has Died

How The Birth of SOCIALLY RESPONSIBLE RECRUITMENT™ Erases Bias & Drives Profit
by Desmund Adams

Published by Focus & Find®, 15920 Hickman Road, Suite 400, Clive, Iowa 50325

Copyright ©2020 Desmund Adams, All rights reserved.

Printed in the United States of America

Publisher's Cataloging-In-Publication Data (Prepared by The Donohue Group, Inc.)

Names: Adams, Desmund, author.

Title: D&I has died : how the birth of Socially Responsible Recruitment erases bias & drives profit / by Desmund Adams.

Other Titles: D & I has died | D and I has died | Diversity & inclusion has died

Description: First edition. | Clive, Iowa : Focus & Find, 2020. | Includes bibliographical references and index.

Identifiers: ISBN 9781734093407 (hardback) | ISBN 9781734093414 (paperback) | ISBN 9781734093421 (ebook)

Subjects: LCSH: Employees--Recruiting--Social aspects. | Diversity in the workplace. | Social responsibility of business.

Classification: LCC HF5549.5.R44 A33 2020 (print) | LCC HF5549.5.R44 (ebook) | DDC 658.3/111--dc23

ATTENTION CORPORATIONS, UNIVERSITIES, COLLEGES AND PROFESSIONAL ORGANIZATIONS: Quantity discounts are available on bulk purchases of this book for educational, gift purposes, or as premiums for increasing magazine subscriptions or renewals. Special books or book excerpts can also be created to fit specific needs. For information, please contact Focus & Find®, 15920 Hickman Road, Suite 400, Clive, Iowa 50325, (515) 985-0400.

D&I Has Died

How The Birth of SOCIALLY RESPONSIBLE
RECRUITMENT™ Erases Bias & Drives Profit

by Desmund Adams

Dedication

To my Lord and Savior Jesus Christ: I thank you for giving me this vision, thought and seed that is planted in my spirit.

To my wife and life partner, Dr. Shondalette, who is both faithful and foolish enough to be on this journey with me, without you, I wouldn't be able to chase my dreams; without your deep resolve and your trust in my abilities, I would have become a fraction of who I am today, and for that, I am eternally grateful.

To my sons: I am extremely proud to be your father. I deeply love you both. You both are the light to my discipline and earthly steps. To Khalil (whose name means "friend"), you are an incredibly empathetic and loving man, don't change. As you embark on your professional career, I hope this book opens up an additional way forward in conscious thought and has an indelible impact on your future in the workforce; to Solomon (whose name means "peace", and who was considered in sacred text as the wisest person of all), I am in awe of your young prophetic, authentic and unabridged truth and how you see the world in a fresh light, don't change.

May this book serve as a foundation for our future generations.

Family Acknowledgments

To Marie Adams, my mom: You are my earliest example of professionalism. Growing up with you as a single mom who had a business focus, you having me, at 11 years old, answer the phone in a professional manner set me on the path of how to live my personal and professional life with excellence. I honor you;

To Doug Adams, my dad: You are the first person I've seen start a successful business from scratch and a vision. Despite moving on from entrepreneurship, you passed on to me how to thrive with tenacity and I will forever carry that lesson with me;

To Jon Stewart, my uncle: I have always admired from up close and afar; you embodied a model of leadership as I grew up; your self-assured confidence continues to inspire me coupled with your uncanny knack for delivering results;

To Andrea Stewart, my aunt: one of the nicest people that I have ever met; I greatly respect you and life is infinitely better because of you;

To my grandfather Albert Stewart: "Grandpa Al", my walking icon at 93, you are the closest connection to my ancestors I have, and I stand on your shoulders;

To my many cousins and extended family: you inspire me. I hope I have and continue to make you proud;

To Sheila Sims, my mother-in-law: You are the sweetest person that I have ever met. Thank you for teaching me how to lead through being selfless in service to others;

To Earzo Lenior, my father-in-law: Thank you for the encouragement. I'm following the program.

To Earzo Lenior III, my brother-in law: Always live your best life and embrace your talents and gifts, the world needs you;

Personal Acknowledgments

To Audrey Granger: you partnered with me in my creation of this book, steadfastly listened to each idea and thought; you helped synthesize it and you were the force that provided authenticity, research and guidance along this process; thank you for helping me cross off a "bucket item" with the completion of this book;

To Jill Fleming: you are an incredible friend and advisor, one of my first supporters and believers that stated to me that my "voice and ideas matter";

To Alex duBuclet: Thank you for teaching and training me in retained executive search;

To Lawrence Richardson: Thank you for showing me and inviting me into your circle of what true success looks like, I am a much better man because of it;

To Jo Anne Weimer: you joined my team in its infancy and you are a main reason why we are seeing the difference that we can make; thank you for believing in me, especially in the early days where revenue generation was a novel and new idea; I am indebted to you and your partner Paul for belief in the vision;

To Aaron Schoeneman: I have deep gratitude to you as you are first person I talked to after my U.S. congressional campaign about workforce in a way that does not injure actors on both sides; you believed in me when all I had was vision, and after tedious timetables, you helped refine my arguments and thoughts about thought leadership; you are integral to several inaugural tenets of Focus & Find and I honor you;

To Natasha Robinson, Esq: as a professor, friend, and someone I have had the privilege of knowing for my entire professional career, I thank you for your input and perspective. Thank you for bringing your years of writing to my envoy as a special advisor;

To All my personal and professional colleagues in recruiting, law, politics, community leadership, corporate directorship and church - Thank you for shaping me with good will. You have impacted me in ways that words cannot convey.

Finally, to leaders, my aim to is provide a socially responsible perspective which will help you better acquire and retain talent; may you be more profitable by helping all people through inclusion achieve their success in your organizations;

To boys like me, who strive to achieve greater than they understand, know this, you have absolute value in todays and tomorrows business discourse, believe in who you are and what you can do! I believe in you! Go get it!

Contents

Introduction

Why & Where SOCIALLY RESPONSIBLE RECRUITMENT™ Matters Most

This entire book is about helping leaders understand the need to switch gears from traditional recruitment and legacy diversity recruitment to SOCIALLY RESPONSIBLE RECRUITMENT™.

I wrote this book much for the same reason I founded the nation's only SOCIALLY RESPONSIBLE TALENT ACQUISITION™ firm—Focus & Find®, LLC. First, I was intellectually curious about the hiring landscape for executives and boards of directors. Second, I wanted to understand the struggles that were being overlooked. Third, I wanted to marry my research findings with my nearly 20 years of retained search experience. The combination and resulting trajectory led to a powerful discovery that the recruitment industry is still speaking the dead and sometimes offensive language of "Diversity & Inclusion". Although I believe the phrase "Diversity & Inclusion" to have lost it's merit and meaning, "Diversity & Inclusion" terminology is still deeply engrained in the industry and business culture so you will read it from time to time in expert citations and study excerpts throughout the book. I explain the offensive aspects later in the book and hope that along the way you will discover some new ways of understanding the barriers to inclusivity and how to overcome them. The corporate community's long-held expectation is that everyone will get on board with the well-intentioned hopes and "warm fuzzies" of legacy diversity efforts with no financial correlations as imagined. The reality is that not everyone supports what "Diversity & Inclusion" has come to mean. While traditional stakeholders take the traditional path, a new direction has emerged. The new SOCIALLY RESPONSIBLE™ direction leads to an organization's bottom line and the language of business—profit. This journey is what I want you to take as my traveling companion. This book will be our guide. I invite you to apply each lesson learned to your business. As we jump into the book, please note that company names are used as examples throughout the book, but I am not affiliated or associated with them financially or otherwise.

My Focus & Find® team and I in laying the research based foundation, reviewed 19 segments of industries within the US Department of Labor. The company considered who had a positive growth trajectory based on The Bureau of Labor Statistics. Next, the team thoroughly researched which of those industries suffer the most with inclusion gaps. Those industries are finance, healthcare, and tech-nology. When I say inclusion gaps, I mean failure outcomes to include more varied segments of workforce across the spectrums of age, gender, and sexual orientation.

The roles of Chief Human Resources Officer, Human Resources Director and Human Resources recruiter are some of the most vital and under-respected roles within an organization. The human resources department is the gatekeeper and main attraction magnet for an organization's talent. If human resources gets inclusion right, workforce productivity, innovation outputs, customer reach, board of director's governance requirements, and ultimately profits will grow as a result.

McKinsey & Company found that companies with the most ethnically/culturally diverse executive teams are 33% more likely to experience increased profits. (*McKinsey & Company Diversity and Financial Performance 2017 Study Update*)

In 2019, Molly Ford, the director of Salesforce's office of equality, told Barron's, "We want to build inclusion," she says, citing company research showing that not only does workplace equality influence employee engagement, but also that an inclusive culture increases productivity.

COMPANIES WITH THE MOST ETHNICALLY/ CULTURALLY DIVERSE EXECUTIVE TEAMS ARE 33% MORE LIKELY TO EXPERIENCE INCREASED PROFITS.

"It is a socialist idea that making profits is a vice. I consider the real vice is making losses."

WINSTON CHURCHILL

Chapter 1

How D&I Wore Out Its Welcome

"Diversity & Inclusion" once was the golden phrase of the human resources and human capital fields. Both corporate human resources departments and talent acquisition firms set out to achieve similar objectives, with the hope of resulting in a more diverse workforce.

However, at face value, that sounds excellent but, following a deeper dive into the history of the United States of America, a series of less polite social challenges erupted from below the foundation of what seemed to be simply niceties. The "Diversity & Inclusion" welcome mat was begrudgingly set out for people of different races and genders. I focus the start of this discussion on races and genders because those were the first long-fought battles for inclusion, long before constituencies were willing to acknowledge disabilities, sexual orientations or gender identities.

So, let's start with what most people honestly first think or hear when they listen to, read or see the word diversity —color. Historically, diversity in corporate America had two major points of instigation—one governmental and the other corporate competition. First, a call for diversity in the workplace came about as a result of government mandates in an effort to get beyond the institutional legacy of slavery in the form of Jim Crow discrimination and segregation. Second, corporations called for a diverse workforce for the sake of competition. Both approaches sound worthwhile and beneficial until one takes a deeper look at who took offense to having to share the workforce. Let's examine; The United States has long been rich in racism.

In order for us to fully appreciate either the government or corporate response, we must first discuss what many prefer to dismiss as a very distant past. I submit that the history of discrimination many want to dismiss is not so distant and has several divisive tentacles existing in present day society and the workplace. Stay with me now, personally avoid the temptation to close the book thinking I'm about to start preaching about racism and slavery. I am not. I will share a condensed history of the past 400 years in the United States. In this condensed form, you will quickly see how inclusion has been hard to achieve by age, disability, ethnicity, gender, race and sexual orientation.

Abbreviated History of Events Affecting Present-Day Inclusion in the US

1619   Slaves in America.

1790   Naturalization Act of 1790; Citizenship restricted to free Whites.

1830   Congress passes Indian Removal Act, legalized removal of all Indians east of Mississippi to lands west of the river. 1831–1838: Indian tribes forcibly resettled to West in Trail of Tears. As part of Andrew Jackson's Indian removal policy, the Cherokee nation was forced to give up its lands east of the Mississippi River and to migrate to an area in present-day Oklahoma. The Cherokee people called this journey the "Trail of Tears," due to hunger, disease, and exhaustion on the forced march. Over 4,000 out of 15,000 of the Cherokee died.

1868   The 14th amendment granted full U.S. citizenship to African-Americans. The 15th amendment, ratified in 1870, extended the right to vote to black males.

1917   Whites attack African Americans in race riots in East St. Louis, Illinois. Immigration Act of 1917, also known as the Asian Barred Zone Act, imposes a literacy test and establishes an Asiatic Barred Zone restricting immigration from southern and eastern Asia and the Pacific islands, but excluding Japan and American territories of Guam and the Philippines. These geographic regions were then home to many of the world's Buddhists, Hindus, Muslims, and Sikhs.

These religious groups were effectively shut out of the United States. The Jones Act makes Puerto Ricans U.S. citizens, eligible to serve in and be drafted by the military but are not eligible to vote in U.S. national elections.

1920   August 18, 1920, the 19th amendment granted women the right to vote.

1955   Fourteen-year-old Emmett Till is kidnapped, brutally beaten, shot and killed for allegedly whistling at a Caucasian woman. An all- Caucasian jury acquitted two Caucasian men arrested for the murder although they boasted about the murder in an interview in Look magazine.

Rosa Parks refuses to give up her seat at the front of the "colored" section to a white passenger and is arrested. In response, the Montgomery bus boycott begins and lasts over a year until the buses are desegregated.

1967   The Discrimination in Employment Act was signed, preventing age discrimination and providing equal employment opportunity under conditions that were not explicitly covered in the Title VII of the Civil Rights Act of 1964.

1978   In Bakke v. University of California, the Supreme Court outlaws quotas but upholds affirmative action in university admissions.

1988   Congress overrides veto by President Reagan to pass the Civil Rights Restoration Act, expanding anti-discrimination laws to private institutions that receive federal funds.

1990   Passed by Congress in 1990, the Americans with Disabilities Act (ADA) is the nation's first comprehensive civil rights law addressing the needs of people with disabilities, prohibiting discrimination in employment, public services, public accommodations, and telecommunications. The Equal Employment Opportunity Commission was given enforcement authority for Title I of the Act, the employment discrimination provisions. Congress provided that Title I would not take effect for two years in order to allow the Commission time to develop regulations and technical assistance, time to conduct comprehensive public education programs on the new disability law, and time for employers to adjust to the new requirements.

2019   The US House of Representatives passes the
Equality Act, a bill that would protect LGBTQ people from discrimination in housing, the workplace,
public accommodations, and other settings. The
bill, first introduced in 2015, would also expand
public accommodations protection to prohibit
discrimination based on sex, and strengthen
other existing protections in public accommodations—by, for instance, ensuring that retail stores
and banks are covered. The bill would address
a remaining gap in civil rights laws: While there
are already federal laws protecting people from
discrimination based on race, religious, sex, and
disability, there are no such federal laws explicitly
protecting LGBTQ+ people from discrimination.
As of book publishing this bill is still awaiting
passage by the United States Senate.

Source: History of Racism and Immigration Time Line, Key Events in the Struggle for Equality in the United States

Cho, E.H., Arguelles Pazy Puente, F., Louie, M. C. Y., & Khokha, S. (2004). Bridge: Building a race and immigration dialogue in the global economy. Oakland, CA: National Network for Immigrant and Refugee Rights. Davis, J. E. (2000). The civil rights movement. Malden, MA: Blackwell. Donato, R. (1997). The other struggle for equal schools: Mexican Americans during the civil rights era. Albany: The State University of New York Press. Gonzalez, J. (2000). Harvest of empire: A history of Latinos in the U.S. New York: Penguin. Martinas, S. (1993). Challenging white supremacy: A workshop for activists. Unpublished manuscript (mimeo). Nies, J. (1996). Native American history: A chronology. New York: Ballantine Books. Norton, M. B. et al. (1994). A people and a nation: A history of the United States (4th ed.). New York: Houghton-Mifflin. Pohlman, M. D. & Whisenhunt, L. V. (2000). Students' guide to landmark Congressional laws on civil rights. Westport, CT: Greenwood Press. Springs, J. (2001). Deculturalization and the struggle for equality (3rd ed.). Boston: McGraw Hill. Takaki, R. (1989). Strangers from a different shore: A history of Asian Americans. Boston: Little, Brown.

As you have just read, the United States arguably carries a tremendous history of bias, discrimination and prejudice that it is trying to mend to this very day as I write this book. Although laws have been passed, some minds have not been changed. Over the past few years, many great thinkers have eloquently stated the following: *diversity is being invited to the party; inclusion is being asked to dance –Verna Myers*. That is a great way of stating the reality and a big part of why I say inclusion is the way forward.

The phrase "Diversity & Inclusion" pays lip service to the greater objective, which is to result in a more inclusive representation of the population in the workplace. While diversity has become an industry term; it has taken on some negative connotations for the white population that also happens to be the primary power broker in corporate America. Diversity platforms and mandatory trainings came on the forefront to counter palpable racism in the workplace. I believe some Caucasian males have felt their leverage and privilege wane and have hated having to face what was transpiring, while the well-intentioned masses espoused the positive benefits of diversity programming.

To this day, there are those who hear "diversity" and think exclusion. To be more specific, some Caucasian males may fear they will be excluded if their environment becomes more diverse. The natural reflex or counter point has been to exclude those who were to be welcomed. This means people of color; older employees and women in general are too sometimes suffering the repercussions of negative feelings associated with diversity initiatives. Research has supported that diversity programs and mandatory trainings tend to result in more of the unwanted behavior of workplace distrust and resentment.

TRAINERS TOLD HARVARD BUSINESS REVIEW THAT PEOPLE OFTEN RESPOND TO COMPULSORY COURSES WITH ANGER AND RESISTANCE—AND MANY PARTICIPANTS ACTUALLY REPORT MORE ANIMOSITY TOWARD OTHER GROUPS AFTERWARD.

In fact, *Harvard Business Review* shared results in a study titled "Why Diversity Programs Fail" detailing how Caucasian managers sometimes feel attacked as if their integrity is being questioned. Legacy diversity recruitment is the opposite of traditional recruitment and makes it clear that the primary aim is to seek out and hire for diversity. This means a diverse candidate is in a downward spiral before they even start at a company because the majority stakeholders believe they were hired to "check-a-box" not because they were qualified. Box checking is a longstanding phrase aligned with to-do lists and census boxes next to race and ethnicity indicators. Hence, that's how diversity became a dirty word and why it can no longer lead the way forward!

Simply put, diverse recruitment has not helped. It was a good idea, but it sends the wrong message. It places the diverse candidate in a position where he or she is identified as a diverse candidate versus as a qualified straightforward candidate. Additionally, it places the client in a position where their professional integrity is called into question because of their companies desire to drive diverse recruitment. Again, this professional integrity question was highlighted in the *Harvard Business Review* study titled "Why Diversity Programs Fail". Hence, the workplace has not seen a great deal of sustained success with diverse recruitment. Moreover, if sustained success was indeed achieved then we would not witness the lack of inclusion that the workplace still envisions. SOCIALLY

RESPONSIBLE RECRUITMENT™ says we value all key stakeholders, community, environment and profit. In short, the workplace should just care about making that final inclusive step—hiring a candidate and "meeting a need".

Strategic Human Resource Management defines inclusion as "the achievement of a work environment in which all individuals are treated fairly and respectfully, have equal access to opportunities and resources, and can contribute fully to the organization's success". Full inclusion is the goal. Inclusion means not just people of color. It includes Caucasian people, as well. I think that's important to say. Inclusion is for everyone. Instead of focusing only on the end goal of a cornucopia of people united to work for a common goal, diversity got off the rails and just focused on counting the numbers of different people invited to the party. Only they never got to dance. Recently, a Charlotte, North Carolina-based law firm – Robinson Bradshaw & Hinson – faced accusations of recruiting African American associates for the sole purpose of acting as diversity props. Regardless of how that legal case is settled, a belief exists that many companies pay nothing more than lip service to their diversity platforms. That's because corporate America has been looking at "Diversity & Inclusion" the wrong way. It has been measuring diversity and inclusion in terms of perceived social justice rather than the metric of business—profit.

"Inclusion and fairness in the workplace ... is not simply the right thing to do; it's the smart thing to do."

THE HONORABLE ALEXIS HERMAN

23RD UNITED STATES SECRETARY OF LABOR

Chapter 2
Forgotten Metrics Of D&I

McKinsey & Company conducted research on a large data set of more than 1,000 companies across 12 countries featuring two financial performance metrics: average EBIT margin (earnings before interest and taxes) and value creation (economic profit margin).

Findings across the board were significantly positive and show linkage between true inclusion and financial growth. Companies in the top quartile of:

- Gender diversity was 15% more likely to have financial returns that were above their national industry median.

- Racial/ethnic diversity was 35% more likely to have financial returns above their national industry median.

- Companies in the bottom quartile for both gender and ethnicity/race were statistically less likely to achieve above-average financial returns than the average companies in the dataset (that is, they were not just not leading, they were lagging).

- Companies with 10% higher gender and ethnic/racial diversity on management teams and boards in the U.S., for instance, had EBIT that was 1.1% higher.

I share this data because it speaks to the heart of my supposition that profit is a direct result of a more inclusive workplace. You will note that McKinsey & Company's research demonstrates that every aspect of inclusion improves financials. An even clearer example of how inviting and including people to the workplace benefits the bottom line can be found through review of filed patents. Please keep in mind patents are a striking measure of innovative excellence and innovation is a direct result of inclusion. Patents are not easy to make a case for or to succeed in gaining clearance for at all. A patent is granted by the government to signify a right or title for a set period exclusively to a person or entity to make, use or sell an invention. In a striking turn of pure, statistical validation, proof exists to correlate inventive thinking with inclusive population corporate immersion and profit. I am about to bring complete understanding as to why patents and inclusion are directly correlated. Are you ready?

The validation begins with a rarely discussed proposed legislation that has yet to garner nationwide acceptance. It is known as The Employment Non-Discrimination Act (ENDA). This legislation would prohibit discrimination in hiring and employment on the basis of sexual orientation or gender identity by employers with at least 15 employees.

Harvard Business Review (HBR, 2016) examined the effect of U.S. state-level ENDAs on corporate patent-based innovation. What it found was remarkable and curious until the ripple effect of underlying bias is considered. *Harvard Business Review* combed through data for almost all U.S. public firms that actively filed patents from 1976 to 2008 and found that the adoption of ENDAs led to a significant increase in innovation output. On average, firms headquartered in states that passed ENDAs saw an 8% increase in the number of patents and an 11% increase in the number of patent citations relative to firms based where such laws had not been passed. It should be noted that these formidable results took an average of two years to payoff following adoption of ENDAs. Other considerations not to be ignored, include ENDA adoptions and successes were typically in firms that previously did not support non-discrimination policies, occurred within human capital-intensive industries, as well as within states with large LGBTQIA populations.

The Chief Executive Officer (CEO) of one of the country's most innovative brands of all time has made it a bit of a life's mission to advocate for ENDA on a larger scale. Apple CEO Tim Cook has written opinion-editorials, utilized multiple speaking platforms and tweets to share his opinion on ENDA and its link to profits and innovation.

"Long before I became head of Apple, I became aware of a fundamental truth: People are much more willing to give of themselves when they feel that their selves are being fully recognized and embraced. As we see it, embracing people's individuality is a matter of basic human dignity and civil rights. It also turns out to be great for creativity that drives our business."

TIM COOK 2013

If you are wondering how ENDAs could have such an effect, *Harvard Business Review* says it comes down to the nation's attitudes and the creativity behind people who are more accepting of cultural differences. In 2016, Harvard Business Review says those who are more likely to be pro-LGBTQIA tend to be younger, better educated, more open-minded, and more likely to come from diverse backgrounds. Those same people are believed to be more willing to take the risks necessary to create inventions. Another interesting fact is that after a state enacts ENDA, more pro-LGBTQIA individuals tend to relocate to that state while more anti-LGBTQIA individuals leave for other states. According to research, pro-LGBTQIA employees produce 30% more patents than the inventors moving out of state.

The way I see it, inclusion welcomes talent and spurs creativity. Working with people from different sectors on a cultural level along with and across the basic strata typically considered diverse can only be of benefit. Gartner, the global research and advisory firm, conducted a study that supports that profitable inclusion hypothesis.

> The study looks at the performance of 3,000 publicly traded companies in the years 2001-2014 across nine measures of diversity. That includes whether firms have women and minority group CEOs, whether they promote women and people of color to "profit and loss responsibilities," whether they have positive policies on gay and lesbian employees (say, offering benefits to domestic partners), and whether they have programs to hire disabled employees.

> The big takeaway: Companies that fulfill all nine positive diversity requirements announce an average of two extra products in any given year, which about doubles the average for a major company (those that tick fewer boxes are less innovative proportionally). Moreover, the researchers find that companies with pro-diversity policies were also more resilient in terms of innovation during the 2008 financial crisis.

1,700 different companies across 8 different countries, with varying industries and company sizes. The result:

"The biggest takeaway we found is a strong and statistically significant correlation between diversity of management teams and overall innovation. Companies that reported above-average diversity on their management teams also reported innovation revenues that were 19 percentage points higher than that of companies with below average leadership diversity— 45% of total revenue versus just 26%."

Study after study proves inclusion is just good for business. The word inclusion means more than just what diversity signifies and that is another reason why using the word diversity will not get the hard work of sustained financial success done. Using the word diversity is a misnomer and cheapens the necessary discourse to be had. Diversity is not about what Caucasians understand it to be—"black and brown" people. Additionally, diversity should be about more than what "black and brown" people understand it to be—getting a chance to interview for the role they know they are qualified for but rarely get considered. Diversity is about more than just difference. The promise of diversity is inclusion. Inclusion should be about driving an inclusive candidate slate where diversity of thought takes on as much power if not more than all of the traditional characteristics of diversity. Because inclusion leads to diversity of thought and diversity of thought begets innovation and true innovation leads to profits. And, profit is the language of business.

PROFIT IS THE LANGUAGE OF BUSINESS.

"Diversity may be the hardest
thing for a society to live with,
and perhaps the most danger-
ous thing for a society to be
without."

WILLIAM SLOAN COFFIN JR.

Chapter 3

"My Ice Is As Cold As Your Ice™"

The crux of the word diversity is that it carries too many negative con-notations. As a label, it sometimes diminishes the groups that companies intend to help. I say this as an African American man.

I know I never wanted to be hired because I was African American. I wanted to be hired because I was the best and most qualified for the job. Most people identifying as a minority would prefer not to be thought of as lesser. People just want a chance to compete for a role for which they hold training and experience. Being a minority sometimes calls for more struggle, even if we are unaware of it.

"If you swim with the current all your life, of course you will think you are a great swimmer because of how far you can swim and how easy it is. However, when you swim against the current all your life, you have to have tremendous strength and because you don't travel as far, you may not realize how good of a swimmer you are."

DR. ELWOOD ROBINSON, CHANCELLOR
AT WINSTON-SALEM STATE UNIVERSITY

I believe some are under the misconception that people who benefit from inclusion initiatives do so seeking a job to be just given to them without merit or having earned it. However, companies do not hand out jobs to unqualified people. They hire people to do a job and measure their performance based on how much revenue that person's work earns the company. So, you can see how a capable and talented prospect might just say, to those fearing inclusion measures, "my ice is as cold as your ice™" so hold me to the same standards you're being held to. Please know that minority groups want nothing more and certainly nothing less.

According to the *Harvard Business Review*, diversity is a marker often ushering in a pall of threat for Caucasian male executives. This group, more than any other non-minority group, takes offense to a vast array of initiatives under the corporate diversity umbrella.

A 2017 survey from Ernst and Young and ORC International announced more than one-third of survey participants felt that the increased focus on workplace diversity overlooks Caucasian men. Of those respondents, more than half believe Caucasian men are being overlooked for promotion and advancement, though Fortune 500 demographics do not support this theory at all.

If exclusion is the fear, let me set the record straight, Caucasian men should be part of an inclusive candidate slate. If the slate is truly fair, then all people are repre-sented, including the male majority population. This is an imperative because Caucasian male executives are more likely to believe themselves victims of reverse discrimina-tion. A recent report lays all of this out clearly. The report was part of a series titled "*Discrimination in America*." The series is based on a survey conducted for National Public Radio (NPR), the Robert Wood Johnson Foundation, and Harvard T.H. Chan School of Public Health. The November 2017 study found that a majority (55%) of Caucasian Americans generally believe that discrimination against Caucasians exists today. For those who say they feel discriminated against personally, are more likely to describe discrimination in the workplace or when applying to or attending a college, according to NPR.

Although multi-study research shows reverse discrimi-nation is not prevalent, the emotional sentiment remains high. What can happen when negative emotions and strongly held belief systems converge; a dynamic of power to forcibly change a perceived imbalance.

Harvard Business Review studied and documented such circumstances where Caucasian male leaders, fearing being strong-armed into diversity practices, take matters into their own hands.

"Forty percent of companies now try to fight bias with mandatory hiring tests assessing the skills of candidates for frontline jobs. The objective is to be fair and unbiased still many hiring managers use the test selectively. In one case, Caucasian managers made only strangers – most of them minorities – take the test and simply hired Caucasian friends without testing them at all."

You know everything about that situation was wrong. That's because the particular testing scenario represents a macroaggression. There are tons of daily microaggressions that transpire in the workplace and the recruitment process, from code words to not being invited to meetings. The reality is that the spectrum of experience is not that different. In fact, candidates or executives likely studied the same subjects and worked at top tier enterprises to reach a point of consideration. Let's do the ice comparison. I studied as long as you did. I lost as many nights of sleep as you did. I ate just as much cold pizza as you did. I struggled with that same professor. I presented to that same demanding client. Someone took credit for my idea in a meeting. I lost a big new business pitch. Essentially, we all have walked similar paths just while looking and feeling different. Think about that for a minute and you'll understand why I say, "my ice is as cold as your ice".

"The eye sees only what
the mind is prepared to
comprehend."

ROBERTSON DAVIES

Chapter 4
The Contagion of Unconscious Bias

Unconscious bias has a great deal to do with known and unknown barriers to inclusion in the workplace. Countless studies of everyone from infants in the world to adults in the workforce demonstrate some level of bias.

Where infants are concerned, research shows we are born with implicit bias (2017 University of Toronto studies published in the journal *Child Development*). This is so much the case that their facial expressions change based on the race of the person speaking to them. Similarly, research shows hiring managers give preference toward job applicants with Caucasian-sounding names compared to those with stereotypical African American-sounding names even if their resumes are the same. In both scenarios, researchers suggest the way to remedy the situation is for the races to interact with one another at an earlier stage of development. Basically, the younger you are when you have the opportunity to interface with a person from another culture or race, the better the response and lessening of prejudicial bias. Earlier, I said unknown barriers to inclusion exist. I say that because a high number of people remain unaware of their inherent biases. Researchers suggest that unconscious bias occurs automatically as the mind makes quick judgments based on past experiences or media perceptions. In contrast, conscious bias (or explicit bias) is defined as deliberate prejudice.

Vanderbilt University defines unconscious bias as "prejudice or unsupported judgments in favor of or against one thing, person, or group as compared to another, in a way that is usually considered unfair."

Unconscious bias is also referred to as implicit bias. The dictionary says implicit means implied though not plainly expressed. Let's be clear, implicit or unconscious bias is the underpinning for most microaggressions in the workplace. Microaggressions are those indirect or subtle discriminatory acts against marginalized group members. It is because of unconscious bias that I assert that some microaggressions are unintentional. Giving people the benefit of the doubt on their bias is part of growing inclusivity. However, it goes both ways. Those who carry the unconscious bias must be willing to acknowledge that they carry bias and be willing to take a considered review of themselves.

The term "microaggression" was first coined in 1970 by Harvard psychiatrist Chester Pierce. In his youth, he was the first African American to play on an integrated college football team but was not allowed to sleep in the same hotel as his teammates.

An example of a discriminatory microaggression starts when a colleague asks where a female Asian peer is from originally. Say the response is San Francisco but the colleague presses on saying, "no, where are you really from", indicating that San Francisco cannot possibly be the person's place of birth because of her ethnicity.

How this becomes contagious is when a majority representation permits this bias-related behavior as the acceptable norm. When no one stands up to speak against such repartee, then the bias contagion grows unabated thus leading to the bystander effect. Corporations and researchers, alike, know this to be true. So much so that, major corporations spend multi-millions of dollars in an effort to educate their workforce and begin to turn the tides of positive change.

In the book *Driven By Difference*, author David Livermore explains just how major titans of industry work to repel unconscious bias.

Left unchecked, unconscious biases are detrimental to leading effectively in the 21st century—whether it's hiring, marketing, or strategic planning. So companies, governments, and universities are investing millions of dollars in teaching staff about the implicit preferences they have for certain groups of people. In 2014, more than 13,000 of Google's 46,000 employees attended unconscious bias training to expose them to ways they unwittingly favor certain types of people based upon their upbringing, experiences, and values.

Implicit bias becomes unchallenged not just because everyone else joins in and shares the bias but also when the bias is interwoven into processes and procedures. That is what happens when the majority carrying the unconscious bias sets the rules and standards. That's how bias spreads to talent acquisition. There, implicit groupthink sometimes takes place. Groupthink is defined as the practice of thinking or making decisions as a group in a way that discourages creativity or individual responsibility.

Groupthink can hide in coded job descriptions, job titles, and even affinity bias for elite schools and elite degrees from said schools. Talent recruitment has been loaded with unconscious bias since the beginning of time. However, it is in a company's financial best interest to fight for an inclusive workforce.

2X

A Deloitte study found that a diverse workforce is twice as likely to meet or exceed a company's overall financial goals. Another study by Catalyst cited a 34 percent higher return to shareholders for companies with more women in executive positions.

A number of companies try to mitigate implicit bias through diversity sensitivity and intercultural training. However, many miss the hard work that starts at the bud of the issue. You've heard the expression, "nip it at the bud". In this case, nipping it in the bud means a few different things. It means starting with an inclusive board of directors, hiring an inclusive executive team, and it means recruiting through the lens of a blind slate. We address the board of directors and executive team in other chapters. For now, let's hit the "blind slate" to explain how it represents a game changer for the contagion of unconscious bias. The fact is that recruiters are not blind to race and gender, but the recruitment process should be for the sake of fairness and inclusivity. A blind candidate slate is one where corporate clients receive applicants that suit their functional and experiential needs without regard to age, gender, race or sexual orientation and identity. A blind slate is SOCIALLY RESPONSIBLE™ because it focuses on including as many key stakeholders as possible with a spotlight on their skills and experience.

"Human resources isn't a thing we do. It's the thing that runs our business."

STEVE WYNN

Chapter 5

Recruitment as a Revenue Generator

Human resources is one of the last corporate function areas that lags in connecting its work to revenue. However, if you believe any of what you have read thus far about the significance of capturing inclusive, innovative board and executive talent, then you see the correlation between the workforce and profit generation.

It's time for SOCIALLY RESPONSIBLE RECRUITMENT™ to better speak the language of business. Financial analysts use revenue growth as an indicator of corporate health. Another aspect of ushering SOCIALLY RESPONSIBLE RE-CRUITMENT™ into a realm where profit is front and center means resetting the antiquated notion of human resources being a cost center. My thesis here is that recruitment should be a noun and a verb, a means not just to an end, but also to the beginning of revenue generating. The time has come to hold human resources more accountable for how the fruits of its labor are actually regarded—profit conduits. Every single employee goes through the hiring process so let's shift the paradigm to view recruitment as a revenue generator. What if we regarded recruiters as we do entertainment or sports agents at the top of their game, finding distinct talent with unparalleled performance worth every single dime? That's already happening but without the respect for the recruitment game. I suggest we respect this vital talent engine for the crucial work it conducts of scouting out and placing best-in-class talent within an organization. Talent recruitment professionals take their time to build relationships with candidates, internal business unit owners, and learn how to ideally match the strongest player for the game being played. If we acquire this mindset, it is easy to transition to understanding how recruitment represents a revenue generator.

According to the *Silicon Business Journal*, the average Apple employee generates $1.9 million for the company. You cannot tell me an equation between the recruitment function and individual employee profit stands far behind that breakdown.

The business journal goes on to report energy companies average the highest revenue per employee in 2016 ($1.78 million), double that of healthcare company staffers who averaged $880,000 in annual revenue.

REVENUE-GENERATING PERSONNEL

Most recruiting leaders get hung up on a different metric —the cost per hire—when the golden egg of metrics is right in front of their faces: revenue-generating personnel.

The right metrics include the following considerations:

- Retaining exceptional talent at all leadership levels will increase revenue
- Longer term retention of top talent will increase revenue
- Hiring more innovators (remember the patent statistics) will increase revenue
- Place high focus on manager-to-employee engagement to maintain strong revenue streams

"The business of business is people."

HERB KELLEHER

Chapter 6
A Company Reflective of Community

We have discussed why it is strategic to leverage SOCIALLY RESPONSIBLE™ recruitment and how it can be beneficial for the company. Supporting a thriving work community includes making the company reflective of the larger public community.

Inclusive executive talent is as important as building relationships to access exclusive executive candidates. It is among the most important factors in strengthening the long-term sustainability of a business.

We are well aware of the fact that for executive designations it is risky to outsource candidates. Outsourced candidates may be qualified but they are not always the best fit for the culture of the company and community, so companies usually prioritize internal candidate sourcing, rather than outsourcing talent. Outsourcing talent is the second step. Prioritizing candidates internally and locally can help maximize the benefit of the company for the community. Once the executive candidates are hired, establishing healthy relationships with them is crucial to encourage retention, and to encourage them to develop their true potentials for the sake of the organization. Maintaining strong relationships will help them realize their true potential and level of productivity. The productivity level of each employee may vary, but it is also difficult to determine their limit without having open and clear communication, so they know you support their efforts and encourages employees to put 100% of themselves into their work. Being on good terms with employees can benefit the organization in several ways. It can help increase company loyalty, professional dedication, flexibility, and the likelihood they will strive for excellence in their career or profession. These are some of the major benefits that an organization can get just by being on good terms with its employees, whether they are an entry-level, middle, senior-level employee, or a company executive. The responsibility of retaining the outperforming employees within the organization is that of the managers of those employees.

Why do good employees leave? This question has raised as many concerns as there are answers. There have been several debates over this question, but the majority of the answers vary from person to person. According to David W. Richard, who published an article on 23rd Feb 2016, a study has unveiled a surprising fact, which has answered this question. If an organization is losing its good people, the organization should be concerned about their immediate supervisor before looking at investigating further. Supervisors and managers are responsible for why employees stay and pursue the company by which they are employed. That also means they are responsible for regulating employee turnover. Losing good employees doesn't only mean losing a resource. The company also loses knowledge, experience and good contacts. In many cases, organizations lose their best and performing employees directly to their competitors because competitors will offer similar opportunity but may have better pay, benefits, or room for upward career mobility. This only carves more ways for the competitors to dominate the market and defeat you in competition. "People leave managers, not the companies" as stated by authors Curt Coffman & Marcus Buckingham. They explain that organizations spend a tremendous amount of money on employee retention to discourage them from leaving by increasing pay, improving benefits and providing better training. However, they rarely look deep into the root cause why employees are leaving. Upon investigation, organizations will start seeing that good employees are leaving due to issues with the manager. Every organization needs to follow this guidance:

IF YOU HAVE A TURNOVER PROBLEM, LOOK FIRST TO YOUR MANAGERS AND SUPERVISORS.

If we look at the reasons for employees leaving from a broader perspective, we will eventually realize that the main reasons why an employee would leave (either a normal or executive designation employee) has little to do with money. It is usually about issues at the workplace. Being mistreated or rudely treated will eventually convince an employee to leave and look for a better opportunity. These issues typically result from mismanagement by the immediate managers, as they are responsible for how an employee is being treated.

Managers who maintain good relationships generally have an open line of clear communications. Clear communications rely on having the diversity of thought in your company to find the correct message to communicate clearly. The modern economy recognizes organizations now have leveled up their workforce and recognize that hiring both genders to increase the value of skillset and thought diversity for the business drives sustainable financial outcomes. Unlike the foregone era, where women were restricted from the opportunity to work in the era of industrialization the modern economy is centrally focused on progressing towards successful equality. Everyone is realizing that it is more valuable to look for talent instead of discriminating against gender diversity. As a matter of fact, it has been widely shown through several studies that higher gender diversity on executive teams increases productivity and return-on-investment (ROI). Gender-inclusive companies with a solid representation of both male and female executives skyrocket past their competitors to success and minimize their chances of failure.

Women are being considered the new intellectual capital as firms that have increased gender diversity on their boards and executive teams statistically outperform those with less gender diversity. It is indeed making a huge difference in the economic industry, and companies that are opting to hire female candidates are excelling in their own fields. According to McKinsey & Company, companies in the top-quartile for gender diversity on executive teams were 21% more likely to outperform on profitability and 27% more likely to have superior value creation. Another factor contributing to the progress of the organization is building relationships and contacts. Building relationships gives us access to the best inclusive executive talent. We should believe in acquiring business partners and empower our ambassadors to contribute to looking for new people. No matter how strong or efficient or productive your workforce is, the company will always need to change with market trends in order to compete with other businesses. There should be a continual search for intellectual capital and dedicated inclusive focused managers.

COMPANIES IN THE TOP-QUARTILE FOR GENDER DIVERSITY ON EXECUTIVE TEAMS WERE 21% MORE LIKELY TO OUT-PERFORM ON PROFITABILITY

AND
27% MORE
LIKELY
TO HAVE SUPERIOR
VALUE CREATION.

MCKINSEY & COMPANY

"Being different and thinking different makes a person unforgettable. History does not remember the forgettable."

SUZY KASSEM

RISE UP AND SALUTE THE SUN:

THE WRITINGS OF SUZY KASSEM

Chapter 7

Diversity of Thought Dividends

Diversity of thought is one of the most significant benefits of inclusive, cosmopolitan workforces. When people from varied backgrounds come together and work to solve a problem, they bring to the table a host of experiences, values and unique mindsets.

Single-culture organizations miss the mark where value and profit creation for stakeholders is concerned because homogeneous culture thwarts innovation. As we already have determined innovation requires fresh, boundless thinking. You rarely get that from a uniform culture or cookie-cutter teams.

My experience has taught me that inclusivity yields diversity of thought. Companies request my firm's assistance with building an inclusive executive team or help with appointing more inclusive board representation. Clients are not asking with help to check a census box. Clients want consultation for how to do things differently. Difference is what comes out of inclusive cultures. Socially aware and responsible organizations see all of their stakeholders and know how the world works.

For any organization to succeed in building a culture where diversity of thought is sought after and rewarded, that company must first go about recruitment in a different manner. It is in the inclusive arena that more stakeholders are taken into account as part of the hiring and board placement process.

In a *Forbes* 2018 article, contributor Peggy Yu, Co-founder and CEO of Stack Education, took an even harder line on inclusivity.

> Inclusion is the only scalable way to build diversity within an organization. Without thoughtful and deliberate discussion and action to cultivate an inclusive environment, all the energy and resources spent on recruiting a diverse workforce are for naught. The employees, so painstakingly recruited, will be gone within three months,

I agree with Yu because I know what she says is true based on my 20 years in talent recruitment and team building. Companies seeking to hire for the sake of window dressing but then not engaging the full benefit of their talent will inevitably lose good talent and money. However, those who seek out inclusive talent and let them get to work outperform traditional, stagnate corporate cultures. Here are some key findings from Business Insider to underscore that point.

BUSINESSES LED BY CULTURALLY DIVERSE TEAMS WERE MORE LIKELY TO CREATE NEW PRODUCTS THAN HOMOGENEOUS LED TEAMS.

A study from *Journal Innovation: Management, Policy & Practice* analyzed the gender diversity of research and development teams from 4,277 companies in Spain. According to the results, companies with more women came up with more innovative ideas over two years.

Another study from *Journal Economic Geography* gathered data on 7,615 firms from the London Annual Business Survey to show that businesses led by culturally diverse teams were more likely to create new products than homogeneous led teams.

My point in sharing all of these studies is to prove to you that inclusivity is being successfully implemented around the world. The opportunity to bring divergent thinkers together to lessen bias and groupthink exists and should be more regularly engaged.

I would be remiss if I did not try to provide you with at least one additional example of a company demonstrating a correlation between inclusion and innovation. In 2018, *Forbes* ranked a company named ServiceNow as the most innovative company. The reason why I share the brand's name is because it has been independently recognized for innovation and holds quite a firm stance on inclusion. The following is an excerpt from the company's *2019 Diversity Report: Diversity, Inclusion and Belonging:*

> When an employee can push their sleeves up during a meeting without feeling self-conscious about their tattoos, we know we're a better company. When a teammate who's a member of the LGBTQ+ community doesn't think twice about putting photos of their partner or a Pride flag at their desk, we know we're a better company. When a veteran is welcomed with a strong sense of community, we know we're a better company. When an employee doesn't feel defined or limited by their disability, we know we're a better company. And, when talented prospective employees choose us because of all of the above, then we know we're becoming a great company—a great place to thrive and build a career. ...When diversity is celebrated, inclusion valued and everyone belongs, magic happens.

I don't know if this entity lives up to its annual diversity report but I sure hope it does. I also hope my firm has the ability to spread inclusivity across a multitude of executive teams and boards all over America. I'm in this business like any other business – to make a profit. Thankfully, I know with my profit comes a purpose that will change minds and lives.

"Corporate social responsibility is measured in terms of businesses improving conditions for their employees, shareholders, communities, and environment. But moral responsibility goes further, reflecting the need for corporations to address fundamental ethical issues such as inclusion, dignity, and equality."

KLAUS SCHWAB

Chapter 8

Corporate SOCIALLY RESPONSIBLE RECRUITMENT™ Pays Off

I spent a great deal of time discussing corporate social responsibility (CSR) in the context of recruitment. CSR is one of the most important aspects of a business. This book is all about linking SOCIALLY RESPONSIBLE RECRUITMENT™ to profit.

A 2015 study by the Kenexa High Performance Institute in London (a division of Kenexa, a global provider of business solutions for human resources) found that organizations that had a genuine commitment to CSR substantially outperformed those that did not, with an average return on assets 19 times higher.

It has been a long time since business experts and advocates have urged businesses and companies to appoint a wider bandwidth of employees. This raises emphasis on both the genders without downplaying the other. Each brings in their unique talent and ideas to bear. Of late, the statistical information has revealed that hiring a diverse range of employees is beneficial for the company. Conversely, the best talent seeks a diverse environment.

In 2015, McKinsey consultants ran a study that included 350 consequential organizations and companies in United States and United Kingdom. The study revealed that these companies, which actually met the criteria of gender diversity, were likely to witness an increased amount of returns and profits. The companies that were able to create a racially and ethnically more diverse environment at their workplaces had even more chances to witness higher profits and returns. A similar thing was witnessed at the very bottom level. Businesses and organizations that failed to create a diversified workplace environment should be prepared to see a lesser number of profits and returns.

McKinsey's managing partner in the United Kingdom, Vivian Hunt was quoted as saying that the data and the design are significant as they include multiple industries and are not just limited to the economic state of the country. She was further reported to have said that the company is sure to experience a rise in sales by 2-4% when the organization makes changes to include a great deal (increased expansion) of gender diversity by even as low as 10%. The same goes for the research conducted by the Center for Talent Innovation. The report said that at least 48% of businesses based in the United States that had a visibly more diverse talent pool in their top management saw a rise in their profit percentage than the earlier year. Only 33% of companies, which had a lower diverse

AT LEAST

48%

OF BUSINESSES BASED IN THE UNITED STATES THAT HAD A VISIBLY MORE DIVERSE TALENT POOL IN THEIR TOP MANAGEMENT SAW A RISE IN THEIR PROFIT PERCENTAGE THAN THE EARLIER YEAR.

workforce, had any increase in their sales. (*McKinsey & Company Delivering Through Diversity*, January 2018)

Many organizations are making drastic changes to their hiring process. They are keen on appointing more women and diverse individuals in their talent pools. They are finally coming to the realization of the benefits that the company can see through maintaining gender inclusivity in their workforce. However, this change and progress would remain ineffective unless the unseen areas of inclusive struggle are addressed.

Unfortunately, women are still victim to misrepresentation at every possible stage in America when we take the corporate sector into consideration. This is despite the fact that women have more college degrees than men have (*Forbes* September 4, 2018 article), as is the trend for the past 30 years and counting. It is crucial that more should be done in this aspect since companies are aware of the fact that the trend of having a gender diverse workforce has stayed at a higher rate for the past three years.

Even though companies are committed to this change, the progression rate has been too slow. Some companies have even delayed it. A study carried out by LeanIn.org and McKinsey called "Women in the Workplace 2017" goes deeper; the study went through the data from 222 organizations that had a total workforce of 12 million, and thousands of qualitative interviews later. LeanIn.org and McKinsey reached the conclusion that progress cannot and will not be made unless the unseen areas related to diversity are addressed. It is impossible to improve and work on anything that we choose to not see and ignore.

Many employees are of the opinion that the representation is justified when they see a handful of women in important positions. They have become used to this fact of status quo and do not really feel that anything needs to be changed or improved. What should also be considered is that men do not really realize the factors and impediments that are often in women's way. They are not aware of the responsibilities, sacrifices, and numerous things that continue to pull women down and take away their accomplishments. This results in men feeling less excited and eager toward workforce gender inclusivity and thus the change is difficult to achieve without that support.

A number of organizations choose to ignore or simply not pay attention to the predicaments and actual situations of those from inclusive backgrounds. This happens after they come out victorious from grave challenges and still have not gotten any encouragement or support. Many individuals of inclusive backgrounds after doing everything and working hard are left to feel at the back seat of achievement. Their achievements are neglected and thus they end up feeling undeserving and unworthy. In some cases, women are working harder and yet must continue to go through barriers and boundaries. Hence, breaking barriers is incredibly exhausting and African American women face more barring breaking and bias in the workplace, according to the *Harvard Business Review*. The following is just a snapshot of how much that group faces.

This includes microaggressions, double standards, and unconscious bias to name a few. A 2006 survey of employees from five large U.S. companies found that women of color are most likely to experience workplace harassment among all groups. They are often held to a much higher standard than their Caucasian and male peers and presumed to be less qualified despite their credentials, work product or business results.

This disparity begins with the very first promotion. The disparity is even worse when women of color are in question. Women still face lack of representation in the corporate setup. When looked at from the beginning, a lesser number of women are given jobs at the entry level.

This happens despite the fact that 57% of college graduates recently were women. The presence of women at every following level decreases and the representation of the women of color exponentially decreases and is decidedly worse. The decrease is very evident to ignore when we talk about senior positions. The decrease results in the fact that only one out of five C-suite (Chief leadership organizational roles) leaders is a woman. Moreover, less than 1 out of 30 is a woman of color. When the comparison is made with the progress that women had managed to achieve in the previous years, it is clear that their progress is being slowed down.

WOMEN HAVE TO WORK IN AN ENVIRONMENT THAT TIPS IN FAVOR OF MEN. ON AVERAGE, MEN ARE PROMOTED AT A HIGHER RATE THAN WOMEN. THE FIRST MAJOR GENDER GAP IS IN THE MANAGERIAL POSITIONS.

Companies and organizations should work toward improving the overall workplace experience for both genders. Women are clearly at a disadvantage when we take into consideration the statistical information that was drawn from close to 70,000 employees from 82 companies. Women have to work in an environment that tips in favor of men. On average, men are promoted at a higher rate than women. The first major gender gap is in the managerial positions.

Moreover, making certain all the major procedures, protocols and processes of the company are convened and conducted in a fair and even manner. Hiring should be conducted based on the qualification and the capabilities of the applicant. It should be based on what the individual, regardless of gender or ethnicity, brings to the opportunity. They should not be hired just because of the employer's or hiring leader's own personal preferences and predilections but on the qualification and the capabilities of the individual applicant.

The attempt at achieving inclusivity and maintaining equality among all employees is effective and beneficial for all. It can have positive effects for everyone. Numerous studies, case studies, and analyses provide proof that an inclusive workforce leads to stronger results and improves a business' reputation and sustainable financial growth. It is when talented employees and individuals can succeed based on their skills and capabilities, regardless of their gender or ethnic diversity that everyone wins.

"I am unapologetic about the
need for social change, greater
inclusion, and equity."

MARLEY DIAS

AMERICAN ACTIVIST AND FEMINIST.
SHE LAUNCHED A CAMPAIGN CALLED
#1000BLACKGIRLBOOKS IN NOVEMBER 2015,
WHEN SHE WAS IN SIXTH GRADE.
IN 2017, DIAS WON SMITHSONIAN MAGAZINE'S
AMERICAN INGENUITY AWARD IN THE YOUTH
CATEGORY.

Chapter 9
Missing Board Members

In the United States, corporate boardrooms resemble an Orwellian scene where everyone looks the same inside and key stakeholders are on the outside begging to be included in the meeting.

George Orwell is famous for his authoritarian and totalitarian essays and novels in his 1900 early to mid-century pieces. Similar to some of that dystopian work, some key voices and potential members are missing from the discussion table, which means their thinking is also missing from the discussion. Corporate investors are beginning to express the need for board of directors to reflect customer stakeholders and the country's shift in demographics.

Many forward-thinking corporate leaders see the disconnect happening when boards lack inclusivity. In fact, one such leader pointed out the detriment to business when boards do not reflect the customer base.

"I would have a hard time even understanding how you can be successful as a business if you cannot mirror the society that you serve in the first place."

PAUL POLMAN, CEO, UNILEVER

Corporate boards of directors in the United States really have not changed much over the past century. According to PricewaterhouseCoopers (PwC), most boards are comprised of elderly Caucasian men. However, California has recently outlawed all-male boards of directors for all publicly traded businesses with headquarters in the state. California Governor Jerry Brown mandated that boards have at least one woman by the end of 2018.

This measure was long overdue. You didn't need to read tealeaves to see change. The global economy has been responding to the importance of women at all levels of business leadership for the past two decades. For instance, women hold 32% of board positions in listed companies in Sweden. The average overall in the European Union is 23% but the European commission's goal is 40% by 2020 for major European companies.

Here in the United States, the California mandate is about more than gender equality because research shows women represent bottom line success when they are included at every level of the enterprise from the boardroom to

CALIFORNIA HAS RECENTLY

OUT-LAWED

ALL-MALE BOARDS OF DIRECTORS FOR ALL PUBLICLY TRADED BUSINESSES WITH HEADQUARTERS IN THE STATE.

general staff. Notice I used the word 'included" because it represents power, innovation, and divergent thought. All three of those words produce positive and cascading effects throughout an organization.

Although some may see California as off to a tremendous start, the move may not be enough to affect true change. Research additionally shows that boards require a critical mass of three representative types to encourage diversity of thought. Diversity of thought is important as a means of avoiding homogeny and groupthink, which as discussed earlier, impedes innovation. As we've already learned, innovation yields profit. If the organization—top to bottom—is not set up to spur innovation then it is set up for financial blunder. Companies that seek and plant inclusivity at the board level, show a direct link to profit. Period.

McKinsey & Company conducted research regarding the likelihood of financial performance above national industry median by diversity quartile. McKinsey found that companies with the most ethnically/culturally diverse boards worldwide are 43% more likely to experience higher profits.

At Focus & Find®, the nation's only SOCIALLY RESPONSIBLE TALENT ACQUISITION™ firm, we have learned that the inclusion problems for the boardroom are the same as the difficulty for enriching executive talent pools with inclusion. Corporations overlook the pitfalls of unconscious bias, neglect key stakeholder representation, rely on old-fashioned recruitment methods, stick to outdated diversity training, pigeonhole recruitment as a cost center, and ignore social responsibility in hiring. According to Deloitte, boards continue to rely on traditional candidate criteria such as a presence on other boards within the industry *(2017 Deloitte Corporate Board Diversity Survey).* Board replacement positions are often filled using current directors' recommendations, or selecting current or retired CEOs as the most qualified candidate. By those criteria, the majority of boards simply appoint more of the usual suspects. Differentiation is hard to come by if you keep going to the same well time and time again.

US boards are comprised of the following:

- 21 percent of directors in the US are 70 or older; in other countries, that number is 10 percent (Spencer Stuart)

- Average age of directors in the US is 63 (Spencer Stuart)

- Directors younger than 50 make up 6 percent of the seats on S&P 500 boards — drop the age to 45, and it's less than 2 percent (PwC)

- There are more directors 75 or older than those 50 or younger (PwC)

- Only a third of companies in the S&P 500 have at least one director younger than 50 who is not also the company's CEO (PwC)

- 80.7 percent of new Fortune 500 board members were Caucasian; of that percentage 51.1 percent were men (Harvard Law Forum on Corporate Governance)

The number of Fortune 500 companies with greater than 40 percent diversity has more than doubled from 69 to 145 companies since 2012, according to the "*Missing Pieces Report: The 2018 Board Diversity Census of Women and Minorities on Fortune 500 Boards*," a multi-year study published by the Alliance for Board Diversity (ABD), in collaboration with Deloitte. Before you get too excited, consider how modest the gains actually are among minority groups based on the following statistics from the *Corporate Compliance Insights* news source.

- African American/Black women gained 32 seats in 2018, an increase of 26.2 percent from 2016.

- African American/Black men gained 26 seats in 2018, an increase of 8.5 percent from 2016.

- Hispanic/Latino men gained 21 seats in 2018, an increase of 14.3 percent from 2016.

- Hispanic/Latina women gained four seats in 2018, an increase of 9.8 percent from 2016.
- Asian/Pacific Islander men gained 25 seats in 2018, an increase of 20.3 percent from 2016.
- Asian/Pacific Islander women gained 17 seats, an increase of 38.6 percent from 2016.

While it may feel disappointing to learn, the rate of recycled placements was highest among this group; more than Caucasian men. This means that again the well was revisited so the minorities making gains were the same ones being appointed to new boards rather than more first-time minority board members. Remember what I said about a blind candidate slate being a game changer. There is absolutely no reason why that methodology should not be employed when considering new board members.

"We cannot solve our problems
with the same thinking we used
when we created them."

ALBERT EINSTEIN

Chapter 10

Fishing in the Deepest Ocean

Traditional talent pools have historically been limited in terms of differentiated choice. Inclusion opens up a whole other level of depth and reach. Inclusion yields an ocean of talent.

SOCIALLY RESPONSIBLE RECRUITMENT™ happens when you intentionally assemble inclusive and blind candidate slates or transparent candidate reviews for clients who prefer a sprint toward inclusion. In our scenario, the best man or woman wins regardless of known age, disability, ethnicity, gender, race, or sexual orientation. Now isn't that a world in which you want to live and work?

At my firm, I went a step further and developed Focus365™ Methodology. This system creates and maintains pools of up to 10 candidates for a minimum of three positions thus totaling three pools. These talent seas uniquely position companies to engage and build contemporary workforces at will and in an unequaled manner.

Focus365™ is

Customized. A custom-designed inclusive talent pool based on client-specific needs in terms of functional expertise the organization seeks.

Focus365™ is

Selective. A pool of inclusive talent that is deeply researched, vetted and accrued by invitation only stands at the center of the process.

Focus365™ is

Dynamic. The procedure is characterized by ongoing inputs in the form of professional development that meets best practice standards. These will include but are not limited to cross-functional teamwork simulations, management webinars, experiential business acumen practicums, and more.

Focus365™ Guarantees 10 candidates who are:

Psychologically-assessed

Focus & Find® utilizes a psychometric tool to predict how a candidate would face challenges and conduct them in a team environment. This formal assessment increases the likelihood of a successful candidate hiring by revealing underlying areas of proficiency.

Interview-ready

Aligned and assessed for the role to be filled. Passes all of the key function tests based on client-provided background and expectations of forward-looking potential.

Hire-ready

The candidate is available and capable of being hired immediately, given Focus & Find®'s candidate profile inventory review.

Talent wins with

Access to the upper echelons of some of the nation's most progressive companies seeking platinum pool of hand-selected inclusive talent. Candidates engage continuing education training on an ongoing basis to ensure they are hire-ready.

Clients win with

A methodology that requires a level of engagement from both the client and the candidate.

Company senior leaders interact with candidates on a quarterly basis to stay on top of talent offerings.

Move our clients' organizations forward with a one-of-a-kind strategy, process and metric that fulfill mandates from leadership, boards and regulatory entities. The most progressive part is what a VIP slate of inclusive talent means to a company—a contemporary and profit-centered workforce.

"All the data we've seen, and all of my personal experience, convinces me that a diverse organization will out-think, out-innovate, and out-perform a homogenous organization every single time. Winning will come from taking full advantage of diversity."

A.A. LAFLEY, FORMER CEO OF PROCTOR & GAMBLE

Through inclusion, everyone wins. SOCIALLY RESPONSIBLE RECRUITMENT™ is the Switzerland of talent acquisition. Inclusion represents the deepest level of neutrality, like Switzerland, where no party has an unfair advantage. This approach focuses on the bottom line profit that results from inclusive talent ecosystems and innovations.

Conclusion

Recruitment is due for a social responsibility makeover. Many within the field have been making gains in that direction for generations. It is not my intention to belittle all of the effort that has come before.

However, the biggest gain of all is to tie recruitment to profit. We're already on the precipice, but just need to equate every step of the talent acquisition process with financial wins.

The first step is to communicate effectively about what the objective is and how we will get there. The objective is to speak one business language for which every business is fluent—profit. To speak a language that does not confuse or offend. This means retooling the word diversity to make it subordinate to the word inclusivity.

This is why my firm—Focus & Find® – specializes in SOCIALLY RESPONSIBLE TALENT ACQUISITION™.

For us, SOCIALLY RESPONSIBLE RECRUITMENT™ replaces antiquated discourse about appreciating other differences just for difference sake. SOCIALLY RESPONSIBLE RECRUITMENT™ brings about divergent thought, which results in innovation. And, we learned innovation leads to profit. Also, companies with a cosmopolitan workforce better reflect customer stakeholders, which increase sales reach, which also leads to increased profit. Perhaps the biggest surprise for Caucasian readers may have been the fact that SOCIALLY RESPONSIBLE RECRUITMENT™ and inclusive candidate slates incorporate Caucasian males, too.

Additionally, you now know that recruitment holds more value as a revenue generator than it does being relegated to the cost center tombs. And, ultimately, inclusive candidate slates result in the deepest of oceans of talent.

My intention was to broaden your perspective about the power of words and bias. I hope I illuminated the value and power of inclusivity over diversity. We need a talent acquisition industry and corporate human resources paradigm shift from "Diversity & Inclusion" to inclusion. Period. SOCIALLY RESPONSIBLE RECRUITMENT™ drives inclusion. As earlier stated, Inclusion leads to diversity of thought and diversity of thought begets innovation and true innovation leads to profits. Hence, SOCIALLY RESPONSIBLE RECRUITMENT™ drives profit and PROFIT is the language of business!

I hope you enjoyed reading this book as much as I enjoyed writing it. May you look ahead to a profitable future full of an inclusive ecosystem of innovative talent.

Index

I

Immigration 12, 15

inclusion 1, 2, 4, 13, 5, 6, 10, 11, 16, 18, 19, 22, 23, 26, 28,
        33, 40, 68, 69, 70, 82, 89, 94, 97, 101

innovation 1, 4, 6, 23, 24, 25, 26, 27, 28, 64, 68, 88, 101

J

Jim Crow 11

L

LGBTQ 15, 69

M

McKinsey & Company 6, 22, 23, 59, 76, 88

men 13, 33, 34, 76, 77, 80, 81, 85, 90, 91

metric 1, 2, 19, 51, 97

microaggression(s) 37, 41, 42, 78

minority 26, 32, 33, 90, 91

P

profit 1, 4, 6, 5, 19, 22, 23, 26, 28, 29, 48, 49, 64, 69, 72, 73,
        74, 88, 97, 100, 101

R

race 2, 11, 12, 15, 18, 22, 40, 45, 94

races 10, 40

recruitment 2, 3, 4, 18, 37, 43, 45, 48, 49, 54, 65, 72, 89,
        100, 101

Desmund Adams

From working at the prestigious Talent Acquisition Group to founding Focus & Find® in 2016, he has represented clients large and small for nearly 20 years.

He made headlines in 2013 when he received a Tribute on the floor of The U.S. House of Representatives by The Honorable Tom Latham. The Honorable Member of Congress stated in the U.S. Congressional Record "Desmund Adams is the epitome of an American success story."

Desmund's company placed 26 ethnically diverse candidates in Antarctica for a client multinational defense company. Desmund continues to provide the same dedication to all his clients, and has hands-on experience with how corporate directorship and executive search intersect with diversity and inclusion recruitment.